Broken People Can Relate to Broken People

Ricky Clemons

PUBLISHED BY FIEDLI PUBLISHING, INC.

ISBN: 978-1-955622-43-1

Published by

Fideli Publishing, Inc.
119 W. Morgan St.
Martinsville, IN 46151
www.FideliPublishing.com

Table of Contents

Broken People Can Relate to Broken People

Broken people can relate to broken people who live all around the world.

Many people can relate to broken people and let them know that they are not alone in their brokenness.

Many people would rather read a book about someone being broken than read a book about someone's life being full of joy.

Everybody is broken in some kind of way, no matter how happy someone may seem to be.

We are all broken in sin that we were all born in.

Broken people can relate to broken people because many broken people use their brokenness as a testimony about what Jesus Christ brought them through.

When we use our brokenness to glorify and praise the Lord, our brokenness will be a blessing to others who can relate to that brokenness.

Broken people can relate to broken people who the Lord Jesus Christ will heal, if you and I use our brokenness to help heal other broken people.

Broken people can relate to broken people who Jesus will heal, if you and I forgive those who have done us wrong.

We are all broken in sin, and can never be more broken than Jesus Christ, who was broken on the cross to save us from our sins.

Jesus was broken a lot more when His Heavenly Father turned his back on Him and made Jesus say, "My Father, why hast Thou forsaken me?"

1

God could not bear to see His Son being broken on the cross, where Jesus became sin in our place.

Everybody in this world wants someone to be able to relate to their brokenness so that they won't feel so all alone.

If you have a broken heart, you would rather talk to someone who once had their heart broken and is now healed.

Someone who hasn't had their heart broken can't relate to you.

Jesus Christ is the best one to talk to about being broken, because Jesus got the victory over brokenness when He rose from the grave.

Jesus was broken for our sins but Jesus didn't deserve to take our place.

We can be so thankful today that we can never be too broken for Jesus to not heal us, because no one in this world can relate to our brokenness more than Jesus Christ, who healed the heavens when He rose from the grave and triumphed over death.

Death is the worst kind of brokenness, but Jesus will heal us with eternal life as though we had never been broken in sin.

Broken people can relate to broken people, whether they're broken physically, mentally, emotionally or spiritually.

When we give our brokenness to Jesus, He will heal our minds, hearts and bodies if it is in His will.

The Lord can use brokenness in many ways, even when you and I might see nothing good about being broken.

No one can ever be more broken than Jesus was when He took on the sins of this whole world.

Many people won't acknowledge that they are broken.

Many people don't believe that they are broken.

Many people believe that they are flawless.

Many people believe that they are perfect.

Everybody has a broken habit.

Everybody has broken a hereditary tendency.

Many people are broken in doubt about what Jesus can do for them.

Many people are broken in disrespect for themselves and others.

Broken people can relate to broken people, whether we like it or not.

Jesus loves to relate to us broken people, and no one can ever be more broken than Jesus was on the cross.

We all have one great thing in common — we are all broken in sin and only Jesus can heal us and cleanse us of them.

We all are broken people who can relate to broken people who Jesus loves to relate to.

You and I can deny our brokenness and try to cover it up with our pride that proves that we are broken, especially in the eyes of the Lord Jesus Christ.

You can be a genius and be broken.

You can be brilliant and be broken.

You can be educated and be broken.

We are all broken vessels in the eyes of the Lord.

We all are broken in some kind of way.

Many people are broken in grief.

Many people are broken in fear.

Many people are broken in disappointment.

Many people are broken in sickness.

Many people are broken in false pride.

Only Jesus Christ is the fixer of brokenness, and no one will ever be more broken than Jesus Christ was when He hung on the cross in our place to save us from our broken sins.

Jesus hung on the cross and died on the cross and rose from the grave with the victory over the broken death, so you and I have no excuse to not give our brokenness to Jesus.

Jesus is the best doctor, the best surgeon, the best psychiatrist, the best psychologist, and the best therapist to give us the spiritual healing that we need the most.

Our broken body cannot depress us if we are spiritually healed in our minds and heart, but a broken mind can hurt and kill us with depression.

Because of Jesus, we broken people can relate to other broken people.

Jesus can greatly relate to our brokenness and fix what's broken, if we confess and repent of our sins and turn to Him with a life of faith and obedience unto Him every day.

Sin had broken Jesus's divinity with God, when Jesus became sin on the cross.

That is why Jesus said, "My Father, why hast Thou forsaken me?"

Even eternal life was broken during Jesus's darkest hour to give you and me the bright glowing light from Heaven shining down on our brokenness.

There is no brokenness that Jesus can't fix, even if we are broken unto death, because Jesus will give us eternal life for being saved in Him.

When God Closes His Grace on this World

When God closes His grace on this world, He will remove His holy spirit from this world.

When God removes His holy spirit from this world, the devil will have complete control over all who are not saved in Jesus Christ.

All who are lost in their sins will have only evil thoughts, evil words and do evil deeds because they will be controlled by the devil.

When God closes His grace on this world, there won't be any more chances for anyone to choose to love and obey Jesus Christ.

The devil will have complete control over all who are lost in their sins.

There will be evil in this world like there has never been before the beginning of time.

Constantly, evil will be in the minds and hearts of everyone who is not saved in Jesus Christ.

The righteous living will not be so sure that they are saved in Jesus Christ when God removes His holy spirit from this world.

God will seal His righteous living children, even if many of them will be put to death by the wicked.

Today is the time for you and me to believe in Jesus Christ and love and obey Him, because God may close His grace on this world today.

No one knows the hour or the day when Jesus Christ is coming back again, because before He comes back, God will close His grace on this world.

Today, God is giving us borrowed time to get ourselves right with Him before it's too late.

The devil knows that his time is very short and running out, so he is trying his best to cause as many souls as he can to be lost in sin.

Jesus is very serious about saving our souls from being lost.

You and I need to be very serious about loving Jesus with all of our mind, heart, soul and strength.

When God closes His grace on all the world, God will remove His holy spirit from this world and all hell will break loose on all the souls who are lost in sin.

There will be terrible times like we've never seen in this world.

We who are alive have a chance to run to Jesus today and cross over the finish line of salvation in Him.

Tomorrow may be too late to be saved in God's grace, so today we need to be spiritually awake and see that God is moving His holy spirit from this world.

If we believe that this world is really bad today, then we haven't seen the worst that will come upon us when God closes His grace on this world.

We Only Get One Body

We only get one body in this world and we need to take good care of it every day, because our body belongs to the Lord.

Our body is God's holy temple for Him to live in every day.

Many people will show off their body by the way they dress.

Many people live like their body belongs to them.

Many people will treat their body recklessly.

Many people will bring danger to their body.

Many people will do careless things with their body.

We only get one body, and we can cause it to be short-lived if we don't eat right and exercise day after day.

Many people will live their life like their body is invincible and nothing bad can happen to it, but a bad sickness can come upon their body and may kill them.

Many people think their body is like a machine, but it can break down with broken bones and pain.

We only get one body and the Lord holds us accountable to treat it right because it belongs to Him, not us.

Our body cannot run like a machine because it needs to rest, especially on God's holy Sabbath day of rest.

We only get one body, but many people will live like their body is eternal.

If we don't listen to our body telling us to slow down, we will do our body an injustice, like locking up an innocent man in jail.

Our body is innocent and only does what we want it to do, but we can overwork our body and displease God, who created us with a body to live in.

The health of your body is more valuable than all the wealth in this world, because if your body is unhealthy you can't enjoy spending your wealth.

There is Nothing New Under the Sun

Back in the Bible days, there were murderers like there are today.

Back in the Bible days, there were homosexuals like there are today.

Back in the Bible days, there were liars like there are today.

Back in the Bible days, there were false accusers like there are today.

Back in the Bible days, there were adulterers like there are today.

Back in the Bible days, there were rapists like there are today.

Back in the Bible days, there were judges like there are today.

Back in the Bible days, there were lawyers like there are today

There is nothing new under the sun.

What went on back in the Bible days is going on today.

Back in the Bible days, there were interracial marriages like there are today.

Back in the Bible days, there were wars like there are today.

Back in the Bible days, there was greed like there is today.

Back in the Bible days, there were covetous people like there are today.

Back in the Bible days, there were Christians like there are today.

Back in the Bible days, there were worldly people like there are today.

Back in the Bible days, there were selfish people like there are today.

Back in the Bible days there were proud people like there are today.

Back in the Bible days, there were atheist people like there are today.

Back in the Bible days, there were people lost in their sins like there are today.

Back in the Bible days there were musicians like there are today.

Back in the Bible days, there were preachers like there are today.

Back in the Bible days, there were astrologers like there are today.

Back in the Bible days, there was spiritualism like there is today.

Back in the Bible days there was favoritism like there is today.

Back in the Bible days, there was prejudice like there is today.

Back in the Bible days, there was Injustice like there is today.

There is nothing new under the sun, just like King Solomon said.

Looks can Sometimes be Deceiving

Some people will look like they wouldn't kill a fly, but they might be a mass shooter.

Some people will look like they are men of God, but might be a serial killer.

Some people will look like they won't do anything wrong, but they might be a troublemaker.

Looks can sometimes be deceiving, because some people will look so innocent but might be guilty of committing a crime.

Some people will look so honest but might be telling lies.

Some people will look so happy but might be sad down in their hearts.

Looks can sometimes be deceiving, and only the Lord can truly know the truth about everyone.

Some people will look so well put together but might be torn apart in their hearts.

Some people will look intelligent, but might think foolish thoughts in their minds.

Some people will look like a Christian, but might be living in their sins.

Some people will look like they love the Lord, but might be hating on someone.

Looks can sometimes be deceiving, because some people will look like they're on their way to heaven when they might be on their way to hell for pretending to be a Christian.

Some people will look like they're perfect, but might be holding onto some sins that they haven't confessed and repented of.

Before We Know It

What we say will catch up with us before we know it.

What we do will catch up with us before we know it.

The way that we live our lives will catch up with us before we know it.

The way we think will catch up with us before we know it.

What we eat will catch up with us before we know it.

What we drink will catch up with us before we know it.

We will reap what we sow before we know it.

No matter how young you are, old age will catch up with you before you know it.

No matter how smart you are, some memory loss will catch up with you before you know it.

Living our Lives unto the Lord Jesus Christ will catch up with us before we know it.

If we live our lives sinning against the Lord, it will catch up with us before we know it.

We live in a world where many things will happen before we know it.

This comes to show that we don't know much of anything, but God knew everything before we knew anything, even when we were in our mother's womb.

What we feel will catch up with us before we know it.

What we see will catch up with us before we know it.

What we see will have a good effect or a bad effect on us sooner or later.

Jesus Christ will come back again before we know it.

We can never know when He will return, so today we can choose to love and obey Him before He comes back again.

Our faith in Jesus will catch up with us before we know it through our trials.

Our works will catch up with us before we know it.

We can choose to win souls to Jesus Christ or choose to use our works for selfish reasons.

Our destiny will catch up with us before we know it.

We can choose to be saved in Jesus Christ and go to heaven or be lost in our sins and go to hell.

Our time will catch up with us before we know it.

When that time comes, we will have no more choices to make if we didn't choose to live our lives unto the Lord Jesus Christ.

Jesus Will Give You and Me Eternal Life

Jesus will give you and me eternal life so we can have plenty of time to get to know all the angels in heaven.

Jesus will give you and me eternal life so we can have plenty of time to get to know everyone who makes it to heaven.

It will take an eternity for you and me to get to know all of the creatures in other worlds.

This life on Earth is too short for you and me to get to know everyone in this world.

We can live 100 years and not know most of the people in this world.

It will take eternal life for you and me to get to know everything about Jesus Christ Our Lord and Savior.

Jesus will give you and me eternal life one day, if we are saved in him who is the eternal life and gives it to all the angels in heaven and to other worlds.

God gave Adam and Eve eternal life, but they gave it up for a fruit that they believed would make them be like God.

Jesus will give you and me an eternal life one day, so we will have forever and ever to get to know a number of people who no man can count — all the people who will make it to heaven and live with God and all the angels.

Have No Power Over Our Choices

Hereditary tendencies have no power over our choices.

Genetics have no power over our choices.

Circumstances have no power over our choices.

Uncertainty has no power over our choices.

The unknown has no power over our choices.

Unpredictability has no power over our choices.

Our thoughts have no power over our choices.

Our words have no power over our choices.

What we see has no power over our choices.

What we hear has no power over our choices

How we feel has no power over our choices.

Where we live has no power over our choices.

Where we go has no power over our choices.

God will not overpower our choices.

The devil has no power over our choices.

Our choices are very powerful because we have the freedom to choose to do good or evil.

Phenomenon has no power over our choices.

The supernatural has no power over our choices.

Nothing in this world has power over our choices.

Nothing in heaven has power over our choices.

Destiny has no power over our choices.

God doesn't allow anyone or anything to overpower our choices.

Beyond My Works

Beyond my works, O Lord, I need Your love, Your mercy and Your grace upon my life every day.

Beyond my works, O Lord, I need Your blessings every day.

Beyond my works, O Lord, I need You so much in my mind every day.

Beyond my works, O Lord, I need You in my heart every day.

Beyond my works, O Lord, I need You in my home every day.

Beyond my works, O Lord, I need You in my dreams every night.

Beyond my works, O Lord, I need Your protection every day.

My works are nothing without you, oh Lord.

Beyond my works, O Lord, I need You in my life every day.

What good are my works, O Lord, if I don't put all of my trust in You every day.

What good are my works, O Lord, if I don't depend on you who can supply all of my needs which my works cannot do.

Beyond my works, O Lord, only You can save me from my sins.

That is something my works can't do.

Beyond my works, O Lord, only You can give me true joy.

Beyond my works, O Lord, only You have a heaven to put me in.

My works have no heaven to put me in.

What good are my works, O Lord, if I don't believe in you every day.

What good are my works, O Lord, if I don't keep my eyes on you every day.

Beyond my works, O Lord, only You can give me the strength to keep going in my Christian Journey.

What good are my works if I believe that I am self-sufficient and can do all the right things without You, who are the righteous Lord and Savior and God.

Beyond my works, O Lord, only You can help me to get the victory over any obstacle in my life.

My works can't give me the victory over my obstacles.

Our actions

Our actions are the best preacher.

Our actions are the best teacher.

Our actions are the greatest lecturer.

Our actions are the best speech makers.

People will know us by our actions.

Even an animal will know us by our actions.

Love is seen in good actions.

Hate is seen in bad actions.

Our actions tell the truth about you and me beyond our words that can be full of hot air.

Our actions will show our true heart condition day after day.

Our actions are a best-selling book with no misspelled words in our body language.

Our actions are who we truly are day after day.

We can change what we say in our words and language, but actions are a language that has the best influence on people every day.

We can easily change our words, but the motion of our actions is real proof of who we are every day that will live.

Beyond all the perfect words that Jesus Christ spoke, His perfect actions had a greater influence on sinners when he healed the sick, cast out demons, opened the eyes of the blind and fed the hungry.

Jesus' actions are more miraculous to people than His words, especially when Jesus was beaten and shed His blood on the cross.

Jesus committed no crime by his actions that people could see, but all of Jesus' perfect actions fulfilled His perfect words that many people didn't believe to be true.

We can go back on our word, but we can't go back on our actions because once an action is done there is no going back.

When I Look at Myself in the Mirror

When I look at myself in the mirror, I will see humility or pride upon my face.

When I look at myself in the mirror, I will see truth or lies upon my face.

When I look at myself in the mirror, I will see good or evil upon my face.

When I look at myself in the mirror, I will see realness or pretense upon my face.

When I look at myself in the mirror, I will see love or hate upon my face.

When I look at myself in the mirror, I will see victory or defeat upon my face.

When I look at myself in the mirror, I will see joy or sadness upon my face.

When I look at myself in the mirror, I will see sanity or insanity upon my face.

When I look at myself in the mirror, I will see selflessness or selfishness upon my face.

When I look at myself in the mirror, I will see life or death upon my face.

When I look at myself in the mirror, I will see boldness or fear upon my face.

When I look at myself in the mirror, I will see success or failure upon my face.

When I look at myself in the mirror, I will see hope or hopelessness upon my face.

When I look at myself in the mirror, I will see healing or brokenness upon my face.

When I look at myself in the mirror, I will see being intact or falling apart upon my face.

When I look at myself in the mirror, I will see Jesus or the devil upon my face.

When I look at myself in the mirror, I will accept who I am upon my face or deny who I am upon my face.

When I look at myself in God's mirror, I will see the sinner that I am with no ifs ands or buts about it.

I Feel Like I was Right There

I feel like I was right there when Adam and Eve sinned against God and were put out of the Garden of Eden.

I feel like I was right there when Cain killed his brother Abel.

I feel like I was right there with Noah and his family and the animals entered into the ark before it rained for 40 days and 40 nights.

I feel like I was right there when Elijah was taken to heaven in a chariot of fire.

I feel like I was right there when Abraham was going to sacrifice his son Isaac on the altar.

I feel like I was right there when Lot and his daughters were led out of Sodom and Gomorrah by the angels of God.

I feel like I was right there when Moses talked back to God in a burning bush.

I feel like I was right there when Rahab hid the spies to escape from Jericho.

I feel like I was right there when Joshua conquered Jericho with its walls falling down.

I feel like I was right there when David killed Goliath.

I feel like I was right there when King Solomon judged the two women to see who was the real mother of the child.

I feel like I was right there when Daniel was thrown in the lion's den.

I feel like I was right there when the three Hebrew boys were thrown in the furnace fire.

I feel like I was right there when John the Baptist was put in prison and his head was chopped off.

I feel like I was right there when Jesus didn't condemn the women who were caught in adultery.

I feel like I was right there when Jesus fed thousands of people, healed the sick, cast out demons, made the lame walk again, opened the eyes of the blind and raised the dead.

I feel like I was there when Judas betrayed Jesus.

I feel like I was there when Peter denied Jesus three times.

I feel like I was there when Jesus died on the cross.

I feel like I was there when Jesus rose from the grave.

I feel like I was there when Jesus appeared before Mary Magdalene after He rose from the grave.

I feel like I was right there when Jesus appeared before His disciples after He rose from the grave.

I feel like I was right there gazing up at Jesus when He ascended up in the sky on His way back to Heaven.

I feel like I was right there when Jesus was born in a manger.

I feel like I was right there when Jesus prayed to God in the garden of Gethsemane.

I feel like I was right there when Jesus was arrested after He prayed in the garden of Gethsemane.

Do you feel the same way I feel when you read the Bible?

I Don't Know Me

I don't know me more than Jesus knows me.

I don't know me like I believe I know me.

God gave me a free will to choose to say good words or bad words.

God gave me a free will to choose to do good or evil.

I can choose to love me or I can choose to hate me.

I don't know me better than Jesus knows me.

I can choose to fight against me or I can choose to make peace with me.

God gave me a free will to choose to be me because there is only one me in this world of billions of people.

I don't know me enough to always control what I say.

I don't know me enough to always control what I do.

Jesus Christ gave up His life on the cross for me as if I was the only sinner, so I have no excuse to not choose Jesus above myself.

Me is a high mountain to climb.

Me is a deep valley.

Me is a trap to set up.

Me is a pitfall into.

Me is nothing without Jesus Christ.

I don't know me well enough to always trust me.

I don't know me well enough to always love me.

I don't know me well enough to always help me.

I don't know me well enough to always protect me.

I don't know me well enough to always heal me.

I don't know me well enough to always set me free.

Only Jesus Christ, my Lord and Savior, knows me well enough to wash away my sins.

I will never know me like Jesus knows me day after day.

I don't know me well enough to point my finger at anyone else.

I don't always know who can change on me.

I don't know always know who can fail me.

I don't always know who can lie to me.

I don't always know who can hurt me.

I don't always know what Jesus always knows.

The devil doesn't know me better than Jesus, who gave me a free will to choose to resist the devil's temptations.

I don't know me well enough to always listen to the Holy Spirit, who will always tell me the truth about me, who Jesus wants to save from being lost in my sins.

No Freedom of Religion

One day, there won't be freedom of religion for us Sabbath-keepers who go to church on the seventh day of the week.

We Seventh-day Adventists will one day be persecuted for keeping the Sabbath day holy, which is on a Saturday and not Sunday.

One day, the Sunday blue law will be in effect all around the world where us Sabbath-keepers won't be able to buy anything or sell anything.

We will have to give up everything that we own to be sealed in Jesus Christ, who kept the Sabbath when He lived here on Earth.

God created everything in six days, and rested on the seventh day of the week, being a memorial day to all of God's creation.

Man cannot change the Sabbath day that God created.

The Sabbath day will always remain the same in the presence of God, regardless of the man-made Sunday being the day of worship that is not written in the Bible.

That day will come for us Seventh Day Adventists to be homeless and put in prison and be killed for not acknowledging that Sunday is the day of worshiping God.

We Adventists will be victorious in Jesus Christ, who will give us eternal life at the end of our persecutions for keeping the Sabbath.

Many People go to Court

Many people go to court and believe that they can outsmart the judge, because they think the judge is wrong and they are right.

The judge has studied the law for years.

The judge has studied the behavior of people for years.

The judge knows very well if you and I are telling the truth.

Many people go to court and believe that they will win their case without presenting all the facts that they need to win.

Having evidence is very important to the judge, who will decide who is telling the truth.

If they lose their case, they look so disappointed.

Many people go to church and believe that they are prepared to win their case.

God is the judge of all men and women and boys and girls.

God is the judge over all judges, who don't always make the verdict like God.

Jesus Christ is pleading our case in the courtroom of God.

Jesus is our lawyer, jury and judge, who we can't ever outsmart because He knows all of the motives and intentions in our hearts.

No one can explain how Jesus can be our lawyer, jury and judge, but Jesus is worthy to be all of these things for us.

Many people go to court and believe that they can fool the judge by what they say.

Many people don't truly realize that the judge is very wise and wants proof from you and me to win our case.

Many people go to court and believe that they can deceive and charm the judge into letting them win their case.

Many people go to court and believe that the judge can't catch them in a lie.

The judge can very well discern the truth from a lie.

No judge can do that better than Jesus Christ.

Many people go to court and believe that they can represent themselves before the judge, who knows that they will lose their case.

Many people believe that they can represent themselves before God, without Jesus being their lawyer.

Jesus is our lawyer, jury and judge that no man can ever truly explain.

Make Jesus Christ Your God

Make Jesus Christ your God, because He is God in the trinity Godhead in heaven above this sinful world.

Don't make money your God.

Don't make sex your God.

Don't make food your God.

They are all false gods.

Don't make your husband your God.

Don't make your wife your God.

Don't make your children your God.

Make Jesus Christ your God, because He is the Son of God and God himself.

Don't make yourself own your God.

Don't make your computer your God.

Don't make technology your God.

Don't make science your God.

Make Jesus Christ your God, because He is the only God who can give you and me eternal life.

Don't make your car your God.

Don't make your truck your God.

Don't make your house your God.

Don't make your pets your God.

They are all false gods.

They have no heaven to put you and me in.

Don't make your job your God.

Don't make your education your God.

Don't make your wealth your God.

Don't make yourself your God.

Make Jesus Christ your God, because He is the Creator God of all the heavens and earth.

Don't make your business your God.

Don't make this world your God.

Make Jesus Christ your God every day, because you and I can't be wrong for making Jesus our Lord and Savior and our God.

Don't make any human being your God.

Don't make anything in this world your God.

Make Jesus Christ your God, because He is worthy to be your God and my God.

Come Very Far

In every race of people, many people come very far in many good ways.

In every race of people, many people come very far in many bad ways.

In every race of people, many people come very far in good morals.

In every race of people, many people come very far in bad morals.

In every race of people, many people come very far in interracial marriages.

In every race of people, many people come very far in good health.

In every race of people, many people come very far in bad health.

In every race of people, many people come very far in education.

In every race of people, many people come very far in technology.

In every race of people, many people come very far in committing crimes.

In every race of people, many people come very far in stupidity.

In every race of people, many people come very far in prosperity.

In every race of people, many people come very far in poverty.

In every race of people, many people come very far in knowledge.

In every race of people, many people come very far in ignorance of God's holy word.

In every race of people, many people come very far in believing in Jesus Christ.

In every race of people, many people come very far in being atheists.

In every race of people, many people come very far in spiritualism.

In every race of people, many people come very far in the Bible truth.

In every race of people, many people come very far in rebellion against God.

In every race of people, many people come very far in selfishness.

In every race of people, many people come very far in loving Jesus Christ and keeping His Commandments.

In every race of people, many people come very far in evil practices.

In every race of people, many people come very far in being lost in their sins.

In every race of people, many people come very far in being saved in Jesus Christ.

Pretty Much Know

Most adult people pretty much know if they are speeding on the road.

Most adult people pretty much know if they say something wrong.

Most adult people pretty much know when they do something wrong.

Most adult people pretty much know when they make a mistake.

Most adult people pretty much know if they are good.

Most adult people pretty much know if they are evil.

Most adult people pretty much know if they are proud.

Most adult people pretty much know if they are using somebody.

Most adult people pretty much know if they have good motives.

Most adult people pretty much know if they have bad motives.

Most adult people pretty much know if they are telling lie.

Most adult people pretty much know if they are telling the truth.

Most adult people pretty much know if they are sane.

Most adult people pretty much know that there is a God.

Most adult people pretty much know trouble when they see it.

Most adult people pretty much know how to do what is right.

Most adult people pretty much know that they are not children.

Most adult people pretty much know how to choose right from wrong.

Most adult people pretty much know what they want and don't want in their lives.

Most adult people pretty much know who they are.

Most adult people pretty much know if they are smart or not smart.

Most adult people pretty much know what they say.

Most adult people pretty much know what they do.

Most adult people pretty much know that they are not animals.

Most adult people pretty much know that there is a higher intelligence above the sky.

Most adult people pretty much know that they are here for a reason.

Most adult people pretty much know that there is a God above them.

Most adult people pretty much know that there is a God looking down on them.

Most adult people pretty much know the difference between love and hate.

Most adult people pretty much know what makes good sense.

Most adult people pretty much know how much they can handle.

Most adult people pretty much know that they are not smarter and more powerful than God.

Most adult people know that unfair treatment is wrong.

Only a few adult people out of most adult people will have a very hard time in understanding what is right from wrong.

Only God truly knows them for who they are.

There is a Story Behind a Story

What we've been through to make us who we are today is a story behind a story.

What we've been through in our lives is a story and what we're going through today is a story.

We all have a childhood story.

We all have a teenage story, and we all have an adult story to tell.

Our childhood stories lead us into our teenage year's story.

Our teenage year's story leads us into our adult years story.

There is a story behind the story.

Many people won't tell their childhood stories.

Many people won't tell their teenage years stories.

Many people won't tell their young adult stories.

Many people won't tell their midlife years story.

Many people will skip over some stories.

Many people will hide some stories.

Many people will leave out some stories.

There is a story behind a story that many people won't tell anyone.

Everybody has a story to tell, whether it's a good story or a bad story.

The stories in the Bible are all true stories for you and me to read about and know that our stories are nothing new to be told to the world.

King Solomon says that there is nothing new under the sun.

There is a story behind a story, but everyone is not mentally and emotionally stable enough to tell their story to the world.

Many people won't tell their senior citizen stories.

They will keep them a secret like it's not good to tell.

We Don't Always Think

We don't always think before we talk, and then regret what we say because it's wrong.

We can talk before we think about what we're going to say.

If we think before we talk, it can save a lot of misunderstandings.

If we think before we talk, it can save a lot of strife.

If we think before we talk, it can save a lot of heartache.

We don't always think before we talk and can end up looking so foolish.

We don't always think before we talk and end up looking so bad.

We don't always think before we talk, and end up looking so ignorant.

We don't always think before we do something that may cause us to hurt ourselves.

We don't always think before we do something that may be wrong to do.

We don't always think before we do something that we may regret doing.

We don't always think before we do something that might cause us to suffer hardships.

We need to always pray and ask the Lord to help us to think before we talk.

We need to always pray and ask the Lord to help us to think before we do something.

Some things we say come naturally.

Some things we do come naturally, but we still need to always pray and ask the Lord to help us to say what is right and do what is right every day.

God gave us a mind to think before we say something and do something, so that we hopefully do the right thing to please Him.

To get to the truth

To get to the truth about a murder may take some years.

To get to the truth about who you are may take some years.

To get to the truth about someone may take some years.

To get to the truth about your wife may take some years.

To get to the truth about your job may take some years.

To get to the truth about your neighborhood may take some years.

To get to the truth about your friends may take some years.

To get to the truth about your husband may take some years.

To get to the truth about your father may take some years.

To get to the truth about your mother may take some years.

To get to the truth about your siblings may take some years.

To get to the truth about your children may take some years.

To get to the truth about your church family may take some years.

To get to the truth about your boyfriend may take some years.

To get to the truth about your girlfriend may take some years.

To get to the truth about the devil may take some years.

You get to the truth about the Lord Jesus Christ won't take long at all, if we study His holy word, which is the truth about Jesus Christ.

Does it Matter if a Book?

Does it matter if a book is short written or long written as long as it has good meaning for people to read?

Does it matter if a book has a few pages in it as long as it is inspirational to read?

Does it matter if a book is short written or long written as long as it is captivating?

Does it matter if a book is short written or long written as long as it is truthful to read?

Does it matter if a book is short written or long written as long as it will leave a good impression on the readers?

Does it matter if a book is short written or long written as long as it is a good book you carry around with you wherever you go?

Does it matter if a book has a few pages or many pages as long as it's not boring to read?

Does it matter if a book has a few pages or many pages as long as it is about the Lord Jesus Christ?

Does it matter if a book is short written or long written as long as it can change your life for the better when you read it?

Does it matter if a book is short written or long written as long as it is very positive to read?

Does it matter if a book has a few pages or many pages as long as it will stay on your mind?

Does it matter if a book has a few pages as long as it will point you to Jesus Christ, who can save you and me from our sins?

Does it matter if a book is short written or long written as long as it is a good influence on you and me?

Does it matter if a book has a few pages or many pages as long as it is a treasure to read?

Does it matter if a book is short written or long written as long as it is a lifetime of God's truth to read?

Does it matter if a book has a few pages or many pages to read as long as it is powerful?

Does it matter if a book has a few pages or many pages to read as long as you and I can learn good things from it?

Does it matter if the book has a few pages or many pages to read as long as it makes good sense to read it?

Take the Bible for What it Says

Many people will not take the Bible for what it says.

Many people will question the Bible and doubt what it says.

Many people will try to add their own ideas to the Bible.

Many people will try to add their own words to the Bible.

Many people will try to take out some words in the Bible.

Many people will try to make the Bible benefit their own beliefs.

Many people will misunderstand what the Bible says.

Many people will believe that the Bible is not true.

Many people will believe that the Bible is not for them to live by.

Many people will believe that the Bible is an ordinary book.

Many people will believe that the Bible is full of false ideas.

We need to take the Bible for what it says, beyond what we say.

We need to take the Bible for what it says, because the Bible is inspired by God.

We need to take the Bible for what it says, because the Bible is the best true story book to read. We need to take the Bible for what it says, which is all truth to add more years to our lives.

Many people will say words to shorten their lives, when what the Bible says will prolong our lives if we do what the Bible says about doing God's holy will.

Leadership Roles in the Church

Many people will take on leadership roles in the church and not know that it's very sacred to God for them to fulfill their duties as leaders.

Many people believe that being a leader requires being educated with several college degrees.

God doesn't choose self-sufficient people who rely on their intelligence and skills to qualify them to be leaders in the church.

God chooses humble souls who depend on His wisdom to lead His congregation in the churches.

Jesus Christ, Our Lord, chose fishermen to be his disciples.

They were not self-sufficient in their intelligence and skills, but were still Jesus' disciples and followed him.

Many people will take on leadership roles in the church and will lean to their own way of doing things, which is not right with God.

Many leaders will dishonor God in His holy sanctuary, acting as if the sanctuary is a place of doing business.

God looks at the heart and not how intelligent and educated someone might be to be a leader in the church.

The Answer to End

The answer to end prejudice is to fear God and keep His Commandments.

The answer to end war is to fear God and keep His Commandments.

The answer to end lying is to fear God and keep His Commandments.

The answer to end political strife is to fear God and keep His Commandments.

The answer to end disease is to fear God and keep His Commandments.

The answer to end greed is to fear God and keep His Commandments.

The answer to end living in pleasure is to fear God and keep His commands.

The answer to end unnatural affections is to fear God and keep His Commandments.

The answer to end crime is to fear God and keep His Commandments.

The answer to end selfishness is to fear God and keep His Commandments.

The answer to end living in darkness is to fear God and keep His Commandments.

Without God

Without God, there would be no science growing up from the roots of God's creations.

Without God, there would be no technology growing up from the roof of God's wisdom.

Without God, there would be no morals growing up from the roots of God's character

Without God, there would be no good health growing up from the roots of God health laws.

Without God, there would be no free will Choice growing up from the roots of God fairness.

Without God, there would be no freedom growing up from the roof of God's truth that will set us free.

Without God, there would be no life growing up from the roots of God's eternal existence.

Without God, there would be no genius, brilliance and intelligence growing up from the roots of God's awesome knowledge.

Without God, there would be no superpower nations growing up from the roots of God's mercy and grace.

You just don't know

The Lord is so amazing, you just don't know how the Lord will bless you and your home for being faithful to Him.

You just don't know how the Lord will bless you in your neighborhood for being faithful to Him.

You just don't know how the Lord will bless you on your job for being faithful to Him.

The Lord is so amazing, you just don't know how the Lord will bless you in college for being faithful to Him.

You just don't know how the Lord will bless you in your ministry for being faithful to Him.

You just don't know how the Lord will bless you in church for being faithful to Him.

The Lord is so amazing, you just don't know how the Lord will bless you in your mind for being faithful to Him.

 You just don›t know how the Lord will bless you in your heart for being faithful to Him.

You just don't know how the Lord will bless you in your life for being faithful to Him.

What Can We Do?

What can we do when dreams are shattered?

What can we do when our hearts are broken like glass?

What can we do when our loved ones die?

What can we do when death knocks on our door?

What can we do when we don't know what to do?

What can we do when the unknown surrounds us?

What can we do when trouble trips us up?

What can we do when the unpredictable trick us up?

What can we do when ignorance pins us down on its mat?

What can we do when life changes on us?

What can we do when our reasoning is up against the wall?

What can we do when time is speechless?

What can we do when our confidence is caught in a trap?

What can we do if God doesn't answer our prayers on our time?

What can we do if God allows the devil to strike us down with an illness?

What can we do if God is not for us?

Before You Judge Me

Look at your own mistakes before you judge me.

Look at your own flaws before you judge me.

Look at your own failures before you judge me.

Look at your own weaknesses before you judge me.

Look at your own ways before you judge me.

Look at your own character before you judge me.

Look at your own life before you judge me.

If you judge me, you will be judged.

What goes around comes around.

What you dish out comes back to you.

Only Jesus can judge me and only Jesus can judge you right now, but there will come a time when we will judge the fallen angels and all those who are lost in their sins.

That time will be when we live in heaven for a thousand years.

But right now, you can't judge me and I can't judge you because we don't know each other's hearts.

Look at your own soul's salvation before you judge me.

Look at Jesus Christ, who was on the cross before you judge me.

Jesus died on the cross to save you and me from our sins.

If We Truly Pray

If we truly pray for one another, we won't even think of talking bad about one another.

If we truly pray for our loved ones, we wouldn't want to talk bad about them when they do wrong things.

We want prayer to change people from not living right, because prayer can change you and me.

Prayer can change you and me to not talk bad about other people who the lord loves to save from their sins.

If we truly pray for people, it will do you and me a lot of good and help us to overcome the fact that we are no better than them.

If we truly pray more for other people, we will talk a lot less about how bad people are.

If we truly pray for our brothers and sisters in the church, we won't be hard on them if we see them make some mistakes in their lives.

The prayers of a righteous man or woman benefit much and are useful to people who want to change for the better.

If we truly pray for ourselves, we will begin to see a change in ourselves and noticed that we want to be more like Jesus Christ.

Drugs Can Mess You Up

Drugs can mess you up, and I know this from my own experience with using bad drugs.

The bad drugs caused me to lose my mind years ago.

Drugs can mess up your health.

Drugs can mess up your life.

There is nothing good about using drugs.

There is nothing good about being addicted to drugs.

Drugs have killed many people.

Drugs caused many people to lose their minds.

Drugs messed me up.

I was young and ignorant to the dangers of using drugs.

Drugs are messing up many people today.

Drugs have caused many people to lose everything they own.

Drugs have caused many people to lose their jobs.

Drugs have caused many people to lose their families.

Drugs have caused many people to lose their friends.

Drugs have caused many people to lose their good reputations.

Drugs have caused many people to lose their souls.

Drugs can mess you and me up for life.

It's a miracle that my mind is restored.

It's a miracle that God didn't allow the drugs to kill me.

Drugs can mess you up, and only the Lord Jesus Christ can bring you and me back into our right minds.

We Can't be Sure About Any Day

We can't be sure about any day that might bring us uncertainty.

We can't be sure about any day that might bring us unpredictability.

We can't be sure about any day that might bring us disappointment.

We can't be sure about any day that might bring us grief.

We can't be sure about any day that might bring us joy.

We can't be sure about any day that might bring us the unknown.

We can't be sure about any day that might bring us harm.

We can't be sure about any day that might bring us death.

We can always be sure about Jesus Christ, he loves us day after day.

We can always be sure about Jesus Christ, who loves to save us from our sins day after day.

We can always be sure about Jesus Christ, He is coming back again one day soon.

Feel No Guilt

Many people will tell lies and feel no guilt about lying.

Many people will use people and feel no guilt about using people.

Many people will cheat people and feel no guilt about cheating people.

Many people will hurt people and feel no guilt about hurting people.

Many people will kill people and feel no guilt about killing people.

Many people will deceive people and feel no guilt about deceiving people.

Many people will tease people and feel no guilt about teasing people.

Many people will laugh at people and feel no guilt about laughing at people.

Many people will joke about people and feel no guilt.

Many people will curse at people and feel no guilt about cursing at people.

Many people will abuse people and feel no guilt about abusing people.

Many people will assault people and feel no guilt about assaulting people.

Many of the Jews condemned Jesus Christ to be crucified and felt no guilt.

Many of the Pharisees and religious leaders felt no guilt for causing Jesus Christ to be nailed to the cross.

God will feel no guilt when He casts all the wicked in the lake of fire and brimstone one day.

Many Church Folks Talk Worldly

Many church folks talk worldly.

They don't put the Lord in their conversations when they talk to people.

Many church folks will leave the Lord out of their conversations, which are so worthless without the Lord in them.

Many church folks will give the glory and praise to the people they talk about.

They talk about people doing this and doing that, without saying one word about the Lord.

Many church folks will talk worldly things that will one day pass away like they never existed.

Jesus is the creator of all things for you and me, to put Him in all of our conversations.

Many church folks talk worldly, as if this world is above Jesus.

Many church folks talk worldly, as if the people of the world are more powerful than God.

Many church folks talk worldly, like the people of the world.

Many church folks love to talk about people's accomplishments, as if they are self-made, when it was the Lord who gave them the talents and skills to make these accomplishments.

If we talk about the creature more than talking about the Creator, our Lord Jesus Christ, then our talk is worldly.

It's always good to love people, but we should love the Lord much more, and talk about Him more than we talked about people who have no heaven to put us in.

Will Come in the Church

Some people will come in the church to get some help.

Some people will come in the church to look for a husband.

some people will come in the church to look for a wife.

Some people will come in the church with good motives.

Some people will come in the church with good intentions.

Some people will come in the church for the right reasons.

Some people will come in the church for the wrong reasons.

Some wolves in sheep's clothing will come in the church to try to deceive people.

Some people will come in the church to hide from trouble.

Some people will come in the church to try to use people.

Some people in the church to start a new life.

Some people will come in the church to try to get popularity.

Some people will come in the church to try to make new friends.

Jesus Christ is the head of the church, and all people should come to him with true repentance to be saved in him.

Can Rip Your Heart Up

The truth can rip your heart up if you are not living right unto the Lord.

The truth in the Bible can rip your heart up if you are living in the darkness of sin.

The truth in poetry can rip your heart up if you are not doing the Lord's Will.

The truth can rip up your heart up if you love to tell lies.

The truth of God's holy word is a heart-ripper for anyone who doesn't believe in Jesus Christ.

Jesus is the truth to rip up your heart and set you free from the devil's lies.

The truth can rip up our heart up so that we can see that we are wretched without Jesus Christ in our lives.

The truth can rip up your heart and rip up my heart to hurt our false pride.

The truth can rip your heart up and ripped my heart up so we can heal in God's grace.

The truth can rip up your heart and rip up my heart so we can deny ourselves and pick up our crosses and follow Jesus Christ.

The truth can rip your heart up if you make excuses for your sins.

The truth can rip your heart up and my heart up if we refuse to listen to the Holy Spirit, who protects us from bringing misery and hardships upon ourselves.

Will One Day Come to an End

This sinful world will one day come to an end, but you and I will not come to an eternal end for being saved in Jesus Christ.

Our lives can truly end in this world, but we can live again without sin when Jesus Christ comes back again.

This sinful world will one day come to an end, but eternal life is within you and me for being saved in Jesus Christ.

This death on Earth will have no victory over us because when Jesus comes back again, He will raise you and me up from the grave if we died before he came back.

So many people have died being lost in their sins, because the good and right that they knew, they didn't live.

God holds us accountable for the good and right that we know, and if we don't live it we will be lost in this sinful world that will one day come to an end.

So many people will die every day, but God's Son, Jesus Christ, is eternal life beyond the living and the dead, and He will make us eternal with no end.

This sinful world will one day come to an end and all of its troubles and evil and death that Jesus got the victory over for you and me will be gone.

We will have no Eternal end if we are saved in Him today.

Tomorrow may be too late to be saved.

In Heaven on Earth

If you feel like you're in heaven on earth, then you can surely thank God who all good things come from.

The devil has caused many people to feel like they are in heaven on earth.

The devil's heaven won't always last, and so many people have found that out too late.

The devil tells us that we can eat what we want to eat and we can do what we want to do and live free from God's health laws and Commandments.

The devil will make us feel like we are in heaven on earth by doing our own will that can make us feel so good.

When God makes us feel like we are in heaven on earth, we know that God has answered our prayers.

When God makes us feel like we are in heaven on earth, we know that God has spared our lives from danger and death.

When God makes us feel like we are in heaven on earth, we know that God has blessed our lives.

When God makes us feel like we are in heaven on earth, we know that God is for us and not against us.

When the devil makes you and me feel like we are in heaven on earth, trouble is right around the corner for you and me to walk into it and surely regret it sooner or later.

Can Only Pray for the Living

You and I can only pray for the living to do what is right.

We can't pray for the Dead, who can't do what is right.

You and I can only pray for the living to wise up.

We can't pray for the dead to wise up.

You and I can only pray for the living, who can move around and go here and there.

We can't pray for the dead, who can't move around and go here and there.

Only the living need prayers.

The dead don't need prayers.

Only the living can hear our prayers.

The dead can't hear our prayers.

Only the living can be affected by our prayers.

The dead can't be affected by our prayers.

You and I can only pray for the living, who can talk to God.

The dead can't talk to God.

You and I can only pray for the living, who can listen to God.

The dead can't listen to God.

You and I can only pray for the living, who can confess and repent of their sins.

The dead can't confess and repent of their sins.

You and I can only pray for the living, who can choose to turn to God before it's too late.

The dead can't choose to turn to God.

You and I can only pray for the living, who can love or hate you and me.

The dead can't love or hate you and me

No One Can Explain

No one can explain how the Holy Spirit works.

No one can explain why the Holy Spirit give us different spiritual gifts in the church.

The Holy Spirit is God, and no one can explain that.

We are so blessed that Jesus Christ sent His Holy Spirit to this world.

The Holy Spirit testifies of Jesus Christ, who once lived here on earth without sin.

The Holy Spirit inspired the prophets to write the Bible that points us to Jesus Christ, who crushed the serpent's head.

We don't know how the Holy Spirit can give uneducated people the gift to preach and teach about Jesus.

We can't explain how the Holy Spirit can give uneducated people the gift to organize and administrate in the church.

No one can explain how the Holy Spirit Works in people's lives.

No one can explain how the Holy Spirit can inspire even a child to preach about Jesus.

We can't explain how the Holy Spirit can use you and me no matter how educated we are.

There are many educated fools, but the Holy Spirit can Inspire simple people to give some wisdom to uneducated fools.

I Can't Trust

I can't trust my mind that can think what I should not think.

I can't trust my heart that can feel what I should not feel.

I can't trust my eyes that can see what I should not see.

I can't trust my ears that can hear what I should not hear.

I can't trust my tongue that can say what I should not say.

I can't trust my arms that can hold what I should not hold.

I can't trust my hands that can touch what I should not touch.

I can't trust my legs that can stand on what I should not stand on.

I can't trust my feet that can walk where I should not walk.

I can't trust my life that can shorten on any day for me to go to the grave.

I can only put my trust in Jesus Christ, who has brought me this far to see this day so that I truly know that I can only put my trust in Him.

I can't trust myself who can be selfish, but Jesus Christ is forever selfless.

Many people love to

Many people love to read books about bad experiences that someone has had in his or her life.

Many people love to talk about bad things in this world.

Many people love to hear about bad things in this world.

Many people love to see bad things in this world.

Many people love to be opinionated.

Many people love to control people.

Many people love to treat people bad.

Many people love to give lectures to other people.

Many people love to overwork themselves.

Many people love to stay stuck in their own ways.

Many people love to talk a lot.

Many people love to watch TV.

Many people love to eat a lot of junk food.

Many people love to think a lot.

Many people love to do a lot of things.

Many people love to stay home from church.

Many people love to deny the Lord Jesus Christ.

Many people love to turn their backs on Jesus Christ.

Many people love to call things their own.

Many people love to show respect of persons.

Many people love to deny the Lord Jesus Christ.

Many people love to turn their back on Jesus Christ.

Many people love to rebel against God.

Will Add Up to Zero

My life and your life will add up to zero if we don't love and obey the Lord.

We can fulfill our dreams and have accomplishments, but they will add up to zero if we don't have faith in Jesus Christ.

We can't reach up to a number above zero in our lives if we don't believe God's holy word that is eternal truth.

Our intelligence, brilliance and genius will add up to zero in our lives if we don't use our intelligence, brilliance and genius to glorify and praise the Lord.

Our Lives will add up to zero if we don't put our trust in the Lord.

This world will deceive us and make us believe that our lives are rich because we're self-made, but our lives will add up to a big fat zero if we don't live our lives unto the Lord who foreknew you and me before we were born in this world.

All that we say and do will add up to zero if we are not saved in Jesus Christ.

A zero is nothing good to hold onto, and we are nothing good without Jesus in our lives.

No student wants to get a zero on his or her test, because a zero is not a good thing.

Having Jesus in our lives will add up to a countless number like the stars, and Jesus will give us countless blessings.

We Live In

We live in a troubled world, but if you have peace within you, trouble can't enter into you.

We live in an unhappy world, but if you have happiness within you, unhappiness can't enter into you.

We live in a greedy world, but if you have contentment within you, greediness can't enter into you.

We live in an unjust world, but if you have justice within you, injustice can't enter into you.

We live in a judgmental world, but if you have fairness within you, judgmental thoughts can't enter into you.

We live in a disrespectful world, but if you have respect within you, disrespect can't enter into you.

We live in a cold-hearted world, but if you have love within you, cold-heartedness can't enter into you.

We live in a deceitful world, but if you have truthfulness within you, deceitfulness can't enter into you.

We live in an unrighteous world, but if you have righteousness within you, unrighteousness can't enter into you.

We live in a Godless world, but if you have God within you, godlessness can't enter into you.

We go Through the Day

We can see, taste, touch, hear and smell when we go through the day, not knowing what a day will bring us.

We can make plans when we go through the day, not knowing what will come our way.

We can go here and go there, not knowing what is ahead of us.

We can say this and say that when we go through the day, not knowing what we may be up against.

We can feel good when we go through the day, not knowing what could happen to us.

We can feel bad when we go through the day, not knowing what could happen next.

We can pray to the Lord when we go through the day, not knowing how the Lord will answer our prayers.

We can obey the Lord when we go through the day, not knowing how the Lord will bless us.

We can not listen to the Lord when we go through the day, not knowing how loving and merciful God is to us.

There is No Measure to Success

If you get one car sold, it's a success.

If you get one book sold, it's a success.

If you get one house sold, it's a success.

There is no measure to success that many people will put a measure on.

Many people believe that you have to sell many cars to be successful.

Many people believe that you have to sell many houses to be successful.

Many people believe that you have to sell many books to be successful.

All the Angels rejoice over one soul that is saved in Jesus Christ.

Saving one soul is success to the angels in heaven.

Success is not measured by how many college degrees you have.

Success is not measured by how many games you win.

Success is not measured by how many trophies you have.

Success is not measured by how many awards you have.

If you save one person's life, that is success.

If you can help one person, that is success.

There is no measure to success in the eyes of the Lord.

Many people will measure success by how many businesses they have.

Many church folks will measure success by how many Bible studies they do.

Many church folks measure success by how many good things they do in church.

There is no measure to success when the Lord looks at your best effort from your heart.

Will Not Stop

Stereotyping will not stop many black people from winning Oscars and Emmys and Grammy Awards.

Prejudice will not stop many black people from staying in this nation.

Poverty will not stop many black people from prospering.

Oppression will not stop many black people from getting an education.

Injustice will not stop many black people from loving their neighbors.

Police brutality will not stop many black people from being encouraged.

Mass shootings will not stop many black people from being good.

White privilege will not stop many black people from being determined to defend their human rights.

Discrimination will not stop many black people from chasing after their dreams.

Being dark skinned will not stop many black people from getting rich.

Having nappy hair will not stop many black women from looking beautiful.

Getting laid off from a job will not stop many black people from looking for another job.

Inequality will not stop many black people from respecting everybody.

Having a learning disability will not stop many black people from using their common sense.

No one could stop God from creating black people to live in this world.

No one could stop God from giving many black people some genius, brilliance and intelligence.

No one could stop God from allowing black people to populate this world.

No one could stop God from loving us black people.

No one could stop God from blessing many of us black people.

No one could stop God from sending His only begotten Son to this world to also save us black people from being lost in sin.

Sickness will not stop many black people from working.

Being homeless will not stop many black people from losing hope.

Being in prison will not stop many black people from being sane.

Being single will not stop many black people from finding their soulmate.

Not having a car will not stop many black people from getting to where they want to go.

Being blind will not stop many black people from being successful.

Being deaf will not stop many black people from having a career.

Being paralyzed will not stop many black people from being spiritually, mentally and emotionally strong.

No one could stop God from giving us black people all that we need to survive in this world.

No one could stop God from bringing us black people this far to see this day.

No one could stop God from numbering us black people like the countless stars in the universe.

No one could stop God from allowing many black people to marry white people.

No one could stop God from allowing many black people to buy a new house.

No one could stop God from giving different skin complexions to black people.

No one could stop God from showing His mercy to us black people.

No one could stop God from respecting all of us black people.

Showing favoritism will not disturb many black people.

Misfortunes will not break the hearts of many black people.

Greatness will not go to the heads of many black people.

Trouble will not always last for many black people.

Crabs pulling one another down in a barrel will not always pull down many black people.

No one could stop God from prospering many black people.

No one could stop God from being happy about creating us black people.

No one could stop God from forgiving us black people for our sins.

No one could stop God from building a heavenly mansion for many of us black people.

No one could stop God from giving this world His only begotten Son to save even one sinner as if there was only one black man or black woman being a sinner in this world out of nothing but perfect white people living among one black sinner.

To Catch Up On

It's hard to catch up on what you missed out on.

Many people go to jail and get locked up for years and years and miss out on their freedom. Their lives get set back for years and years, and they can't experience driving a car, shopping at the stores and living in a house.

Many people are sick for years and years and miss out on good health that feels so good to healthy people.

It's hard to catch up on what you missed out on, and you'll surely regret it.

Many people leave their family and miss out on especially their children by not being there in their lives to see them grow up, which is a beautiful thing to see.

It's hard to catch up on what you missed out on, and it can set you back in the misery of feeling left behind in time.

The beauty about giving your life to the Lord is that it's like you never missed out on living your life unto Him.

If you decide to live your life unto the Lord, it's not hard to catch up on living a Christian life.

When you live for Jesus, you won't miss out on living in sin, which is easy to catch up on because we were born in sin.

We Only Know

We only know what is going on in this world.

We don't know what is going on in heaven.

We can only believe that there is no law-breaking in heaven.

We can only believe that there is no immorality in heaven.

We can only believe that there is no grief in heaven.

We can only believe that there is no sin in heaven.

We only know what is going on in this world.

We don't know what is going on in heaven.

We can only believe that heaven is a perfect place to live in.

We can only believe that heaven is a great place to live in.

We can only believe that heaven is a happy place to live in.

We only know what is going on in this world.

We don't know what is going on in other worlds.

Heaven knows what is going on in this sinful world.

Other worlds know what is going on in this sinful world.

Because of having a sinful nature, we have a lack of knowledge and don't know what is going on in heaven and other worlds because they're far more advanced in knowledge than this world.

There are People Who Will

There are people who will kill people and will believe that God told them to do it.

There are people who will kidnap people and will believe that God told them to do it.

There are people who will rob people and will believe that God told them to do it.

God will not tempt anyone to do evil.

God will not tell anyone to kill people.

God will not tell anyone to kidnap people.

God will not tell anyone to rob people.

God will not tell anyone to do something wrong.

God will not tell anyone to do something bad.

There are people who don't believe that there is a devil.

The devil is the one who tempts people to do evil.

The devil is evil all the time and tries to tempt you and me to do evil.

There are people who will do evil things and will believe that God told them to do those evil things.

The Devil is a murderer, thief and a liar every day, but God is holy and righteous and does no evil.

God is good all the time, but the devil has his human agents to do evil.

Good Christians believe that God is for them and not against them.

God is All-Powerful

God is all-powerful and is the source of power over all of His creations.

God is the source of power, not the zodiac signs that have no power to give you and me the victory over troubled times in our lives.

God is the origin of power, not the government that will fail without God.

God is all-powerful and rules over the heavens and the earth, which is under God's kingship.

God is the source of power, not spiritualism, which has no power to raise the dead like God's Son Jesus Christ will do when He comes back again to raise the righteous dead and change the righteous living from mortal to immortal in the twinkling of an eye.

God is the origin of power, not education, technology and science that didn't exist before God, who allowed this world to greatly advanced in civilization.

God is all-powerful, and limits the devil's power of temptation over us, who can call on the Lord to give us the power to resist the devil's temptations.

Cover up

Many people will cover up how they truly feel.

They won't talk about how they truly feel and keep it all bottled up on the inside.

Many people believe that they will be criticized for telling someone how they truly feel.

Many people believe that they will be looked down on for telling someone how they truly feel.

Many people believe that they will be rejected for telling someone how they truly feel.

Many people believe that they will be talked bad about for telling someone how they truly feel.

Many people will cover up how they truly feel, but it is always a good thing to tell Jesus how we feel.

You and I can believe that Jesus won't criticize us for telling Him how we truly feel.

You and I can always believe that Jesus won't be against us for telling him how we truly feel about anything.

Covering up how we truly feel can be a good thing because we don't want to tell it to the wrong people.

There is Nothing Funny About Sin

Many people will say some words that are not good and will try to be funny, even though what they say may be an offensive

There is nothing funny about sinful words that can sound good to people who are living in sin.

Many people will say careless clever words and feel no guilt, as if they were saying the right words, and then they walk away feeling good.

Many people will joke on someone in a nice way and believe that they are right about their joke, when there is nothing funny about sin.

Many people will joke and be serious about what they say from their heart, and someone else may laugh and find it to be funny.

There is nothing funny about sin, and the Lord will always see that there is no joke when you and I laugh at sin because sin is so deadly, like a poisonous snake.

We Can't Overlook Sin

We can't overlook sin like it is as light as a feather floating in the air, because sin is very heavy and can crush our skulls.

We can't overlook sin like it is a bird flying so free in the sky, because it's like an oil spill that a bird can land in and drown.

We can't overlook sin like it is a baby lying down in the crib, because sin is like a milk snake crawling towards the baby's crib.

We can't overlook sin like it is a beautiful warm sunny day, because sin is like a bad storm moving in with tornadoes.

We can't overlook sin like it is good ground to grow a garden in, because sin is like an earthquake that will shake up and break up the ground and will take down our house with you and me in it

We can't overlook sin like it is a normal thing, because sin is disarranged and filled with nothing but confusion.

We can't overlook sin in the church, because sin is a liar in character.

We can't overlook sin in our lives, because sin will lay a trap for us to fall into.

We can't overlook sin in this world, because Jesus Christ gave up His life on the cross for the sins of the world.

God does not overlook sin, he looks at it under a microscope.

Very Seriously

Many church folks don't take their faith in Jesus Christ very seriously.

They want to always live a comfortable life without going through any trial for Jesus' holy name sake.

Many church folks don't take going to church very seriously.

They go to church when they feel like going, not because the Lord says to assemble yourselves together in the household of faith.

Many church folks don't take the holy Sabbath day very seriously.

They do their own things, as if the Sabbath day is no different from any other day of the week.

Many church folks don't take returning tithes and offerings very seriously.

They hold onto the one-tenth of earnings like it's their own to keep.

They want God to bless them while they rob God.

Many church folks don't take God's health message very seriously.

They want God to bless their health, while they reject God's health plan for them to live a long life.

Many church folks don't take being a Christian very seriously.

They say that they are a Christians while they break God's Commandments, as if God's Commandments are worthless and can be walked all over like a carpet on the floor.

Words Can Be

Words can be good.

Words can be bad.

Words can be clever.

Words can be deceiving.

Words can be honest.

Words can be true.

Words can be false.

Words can be wonderful.

Words can be deep.

Words can be encouraging.

Words can be discouraging.

Words can be disappointing.

Words can be uplifting.

Words can be right.

Words can be wrong.

Words can be dishonest.

Words can be happy.

Words can be sad.

Words can be careful.

Words can be tactful.

Words can be defensive.

Words can be respectful.

Words can be disrespectful.

Words can be fast.

Words can be slow.

Words can be angry.

Words can be mean.

Words can be smooth.

Words can be loud.

Words can be soft.

Words can be funny.

Words can be memorable.

Words can be exciting.

Words can be boring.

Words can be evil.

Words can be spiritual.

Words can be filled with strife.

Words can be life.

Words can be death.

Words can be jealous.

Words can be trouble.

Words can be important.

Words can be little.

Words can be great.

Words can be rowdy.

Words can be righteous.

Words can be changeable.

Words can be worrisome.

Words can be amusing.

Words can be loving.

Words can be hateful.

Words can be beautiful.

Words can be ugly.

Words can be cheerful.

Words can be positive.

Words can be negative.

Words can be brilliant.

Words to be thoughtful.

Words can be disagreeable.

Words can be agreeable.

Words can be empty.

Words can be meaningful.

Words can be stressful.

Words can be bondage.

Words can be freedom.

Words can be trash.

Words can be convincing.

Words can be comfort.

Words can be dangerous.

Words can be strong.

Words can be weak.

Words can be grateful.

Words can be cruel.

Words can be swift.

Words can be refined.

Words can be crazy.

Words can be difficult.

Words can be misunderstood.

Words can be on time.

Words can be too late.

Words can be reliable.

Words can be unreliable.

Words can be superb.

Words can be reckless.

Words can be moving.

Words can be penetrated.

Words can be not believable.

Words in the Bible can always be believable about Jesus Christ, who is the word of God.

Words can be sure.

Words can be rude.

Words can be certain.

Words can be envied.

Words can be conniving.

Words can be war.

Words can be inspiring.

Words can be motivating.

Words can be mysterious.

Words can be clear.

Words can be confusing.

Words can be a blessing.

Words can be a curse.

Words can be helpful.

Words can be hurtful.

Words to be cherishing.

Words can be powerful.

Words can be soothing.

Words can be correct.

Words can be incorrect.

Words can be dividing.

Words can be unity.

Words can be speechless.

Words can be normal.

Words can be abnormal.

Words can be bold.

Words can be fearful.

Words can be ignored.

Words can be accepted.

Words can be rejected.

Words can be like heaven.

Words can be like hell.

Words can be seductive.

Words can be careless.

Words can be intelligent.

Words can be rioting.

Words can be genius.

Words can be knowledge.

Words can be civilized.

Words can be barbaric.

Words can be Hasty.

Words can be appealing.

Words can be destructive.

Words can be sensible.

Words can be uncontrolled.

Words can be controlled.

Words can be silenced.

Words can be troublesome.

Words can be victorious.

Words can be cold.

Words can be ill.

Words can be honored.

Words can be heard.

Words can be thankful.

Words can be explained.

Words can be reported.

Words can be persuasive.

Words can be argumentative.

Words can be final.

Words can be understood.

Words can be proclaimed.

Words can be distinct.

Words can be rugged.

Words can be satisfying.

Words can be unstable.

Words can be stable.

Words can be sanctified by God.

Words can be direct.

Words can be indirect.

Words can be provoking.

Words can be depressing.

Words can be bullying.

Words can be competitive.

Words can be extreme.

Words can be insane.

Words can be sane.

Words can be educational.

Words can be back and forth.

Words can be compromised.

Words can be uncompromised.

Words can be a vow.

Words can be peaceful.

Words can be fair.

Words can be preached.

Words can spread the gospel of Jesus Christ.

It Will Follow You Around

If you are good, it will follow you around.

If you are bad, it will follow you around.

If you are honest, it will follow you around.

If you are smart, it will follow you around.

If you are stupid, it will follow you around.

If you're educated, it will follow you around.

If you are wise, it will follow you around.

If you are friendly, it will follow you around.

If you are mean, it will follow you around.

If you are poor, it will follow you around.

If you are rich, it will follow you around.

If you are loving, it will follow you around.

If you are hateful, it will follow you around.

If you are proud, it will follow you around.

If you are humble, it will follow you around.

If you are confident, it will follow you around.

If you are fearful, it will follow you around.

If you are a Christian, it will follow you around.

If you are faithful, it will follow you around.

If you are ignorant, it will follow you around.

If you are talkative, it will follow you around.

If you are quiet, it will follow you around.

If you are careful, it will follow you around.

If you are prejudiced, it will follow you around.

If you are judgmental, it will follow you around.

If you are forgiving, it will follow you around.

If you love Jesus Christ, it will follow you around.

If you live right, it will follow you around.

If you are respectful, it will follow you around.

If you are kind, it will follow you around.

If you are healthy, it will follow you around.

If you are sick, it will follow you around.

If you are strong, it will follow you around.

If you are weak, it will follow you around.

If you are a liar, it will follow you around.

If you are happy, it will follow you around.

If you are sad, it will follow you around.

If you treat people right, it will follow you around.

If you are discontent, it will follow you around.

If you are greedy, it will follow you around.

If you are content, it will follow you around.

If you know the Bible scriptures, it will follow you around.

If you stay in prayer, it will follow you around.

If you keep God's Commandments, it will follow you around.

Memories

Memories are like having another pair of eyes that only see what's in our minds.

Memories are like living in another life in our minds.

Memories are like watching a movie in our minds.

Memories are like seeing dead loved ones who are only alive in our minds.

Memories are like seeing pictures of people only in our minds.

Memories can be short, like a green light turning red.

Memories can be short, like a commercial on TV.

Memories can be short, like turning over a page in a book.

Memories can be long, like driving to another city.

Memories can be long, like rain water running down a drain.

Memories can be long, like digging a deep hole in the ground.

Memories can be good, like the sun rising in the early morning.

Memories can be good, like getting a good night's sleep.

Memories can be good, like graduating from college.

Memories can be good, like buying a new house.

Memories can be bad, like getting a flat tire.

Memories can be bad, like back pain.

Memories can be bad, like a nightmare.

Memories of when we first got baptized in the church are lasting memories of accepting Jesus Christ to be our Lord and Savior.

Memories of where the Lord brought us from are lasting memories for you and me to be very thankful unto the Lord.

Memories of those who left the church are sorrowful memories.

Memories of our trials for Jesus' name sake are victorious memories about Jesus never failing us through our trials.

Memories are like fire burning the woods of our thoughts.

We can think on memories that can burn like fire in our minds.

Memories are like a river flowing in our minds.

Bad memories are like a storm in our minds.

God will closely watch our memories in the household of faith, where our memories are sealed in God's grace.

The Truth is Not Popular

The truth is not popular with many people who don't like the truth.

The truth will not make many friends, even though the truth is very friendly to everyone.

The truth is not popular and will not get many followers.

The truth will make more enemies than friends.

The truth is not popular.

In the courtroom, a judge and the jury love the truth to be popular in the courtroom, but lies have won the popularity contest in some courtrooms.

The truth is Jesus Christ, who is not popular in this sinful world.

The truth never has been popular in this world where lies are very popular every day.

The truth is not popular in the government.

The truth is not popular in many bookstores.

The truth is not popular in many marriages.

The truth is not popular in many colleges.

The truth is not popular in many schools.

Lucifer tried to make his lies popular in heaven.

The devil has made his lies very popular in this world.

The truth is not popular to anyone who doesn't love the truth.

The truth is not popular to anyone who won't accept the truth.

The truth is like a nerd to many people who look down on nerds because they're not popular.

The truth is a warrior, not a nerd.

The truth is a warrior in genius, brilliance and social skills every day.

The truth is a warrior that a lie can't kill.

The truth is not popular in this world, but the truth is always victorious.

Jesus Christ gave us proof of this when He rose from the grave, triumphing over lying death and the lying grave.

Eternal life is the truth in Jesus Christ, and death and the grave know that to be the truth.

The truth is not popular in this world where lies love to wrestle with the truth, but lies will never pin down the truth.

It is Not Too Hard for Jesus

Your life and my life are not too hard for Jesus to change our lives for us to live for Him.

If you are a liar, confess and repent of your sins and come to Jesus.

If you are a murderer, confess and repent of your sins and come to Jesus.

If you are an adulterer confess and repent of your sins and come to Jesus.

Your life and my life are not too hard for Jesus Christ to bless our lives if we come to Him.

If you are a thief, confess and repent of your sins and come to Jesus.

If you are a homosexual, confess and repent of your sins and come to Jesus.

Your life and my life are not too hard for Jesus to change if we live our lives obeying Him.

If you are a pretender, confess and repent of your sins and come to Jesus.

If you are an abuser, confess and repent of your sins and come to Jesus.

If you are an alcoholic, confess and repent of your sins and come to Jesus.

Your life and my life are not too hard for Jesus to change if we live our lives giving Him the glory and praise.

If you are a gossiper, confess and repent of your sins and come to Jesus.

If you are a critic, confess and repent of your sins and come to Jesus.

If you are proud, confess and repent of your sins and come to Jesus.

If you are a complainer, confess and repent of your sins and come to Jesus.

Your life and my life are not too hard for Jesus to change so that we live our lives doing His holy will.

If you are prejudiced, confess and repent of your sins and come to Jesus.

If you are a glutton, confess and repent of your sins and come to Jesus.

If you are bitter, confess and repent of your sins and come to Jesus.

If you are negative, confess and repent of your sins and come to Jesus.

Your life and my life are not too hard for Jesus to change our lives and give us joy.

If you are a troublemaker, confess and repent of your sins and come to Jesus.

Your life and my life are not too hard for Jesus to change for the better so that we can worship and serve Him.

Are Great At

Many people are great at telling lies.

A few people are great at telling the truth.

Many people are great at talking.

A few people are great at listening.

Many people are great at being judgmental.

Many people are great at being selfish.

A few people are great at being selfless.

Many people are great at being foolish.

A few people are great at being wise.

Many people are great at being ignorant.

Many people are great at being intelligent.

Many people are great at having a straight-faced look.

A few people are great at smiling.

Many people are great at being lazy

A few people are great at working hard.

Many women are great at looking beautiful.

A few women are great at having good character.

Many people are great at being unfair.

A few people are great at being fair.

Many people are great at being mean.

A few people are great at being nice.

Many people are great at being bad.

A few people are great at being good.

Jesus Christ is great at loving everybody.

A few people are great at loving God.

God's Son, Jesus Christ, is great at saving everybody from their sins.

A few people are great at confessing and repenting of their sins unto Jesus Christ.

Many people are great at rebelling against God.

A few people are great at keeping God's holy law.

Many people are great at being rude.

A few people are great at being polite.

Many people are great at being disrespectful.

A few people are great at being respectful.

Many people are great at not doing what they say.

A few people are great at doing what they say.

Many people are great at believing what they want to believe.

A few people are great at believing the truth.

Many people are great at pretending.

A few people are great at being real.

Many people are great at being proud.

A few people are great at being humble.

Many people are great at pointing their fingers at other people's flaws.

A few people are great at seeing their own flaws.

Many people are great at not wanting to change from their evil ways.

A few people are great at changing to do good.

Many people are great at speeding on the road.

A few people are great at driving the speed limit.

Many people are great at going to church.

A few people are great at loving all of their brothers and sisters in the church.

Many people are great at criticizing the church.

A few people are great at building up the church.

Many people are great at not going to church.

A few people are great at loving Jesus Christ, who is the head of the church.

Many people are great at leaving the church.

A few people are great at being the church bride of Jesus Christ.

Many people are great at being corrupt.

A few people are great at good morals.

Many people are great at self-ambition.

A few people are great at showing interest in others.

Many people are great at doing their own will.

A few people are great at doing God's holy will.

For What is Right

If we don't stand up for what is right, we will fall for what is wrong.

What may be right to me, might be wrong to you.

God's holy word is always right for you and me to stand up for what is right In God's holy word.

Many people will use God's holy word in the wrong way, using it as an excuse for their own selfish desires.

If we don't stand up for what is right, we will fall into corruption.

There are people who love to please people rather than please God.

Many people will put people first in their lives and will put God last in their lives.

Many people won't stand up for what's right by God.

If they see you and me stand up for what's right, they believe that we are wrong.

They believe that we don't know what we are doing.

They believe that something is wrong with you and me.

Many people in the church don't know what is right to stand up for.

They take on the traditions of this world and live by that rather than living by God's holy word.

Many people will invent their own made up Bible and will stand up for what they believe to be right by what they say, not by being in line with God's holy word.

Many people will make up their own scriptures that are not holy and were not inspired by God.

Many people will make up their own rights and wrongs that are so different from what the Bible says.

If you and I don't stand up for what is right by God's holy word, we will sooner or later regret it and be no witness of Jesus Christ to unbelievers.

If you and I don't stand up for what is right and what we believe, we will fall down in a lost cause having no righteousness unto the Lord.

There is no wrong in right, but many people will try to make wrong into right and use the Lord's name to make their wrongs right.

If you and I don't stand up for what is right by God's holy word, we will sooner or later fall by the wayside and not even see it, all the while believing that we are right with God.

Made in the USA
Middletown, DE
14 August 2022

70512971R00056